Stocks

Beginners Manual to invest wisely using simple but effective trading strategies

Table of Contents

Introduction

Tired of working at a meaningless job that has failed to provide you with the kind of financial freedom you desired and looking for some other ways to earn? In today's rapidly changing world, it is practically impossible to survive on a single source of income. You need more than one source of income. We have the perfect solution to your troubles.

In this book, we will tell you how to own a business; yes becoming a business owner. If you still haven't guessed, we are talking about "Stocks". Stocks are the right option for you to increase your wealth and becoming a business owner. I am sure you have heard many things about stocks, about how they are highly uncertain and risky. Some of it is true but it doesn't mean you cannot make money.

We will teach some of the best strategies formulated by the experts to make high earnings from stocks and avoid losing money. There are many strategies which if used cleverly can help you get great returns on your investment. Each of these strategies have been broken down into parts to make it easier for you to understand it. In this book, you will first learn the basic definition of the stocks and its major types. Next we will teach you how to read a stock quote. Once you are acquainted with it, we will then tell you how to actually buy a stock from the stock market.

Once you have read this book, you will be all ready to buy your stock. Unlike many people who just invest in stocks based on speculations, you will actually be able to make a right decision about the most suitable company to invest in using both the strategies we will teach you and your instincts. So stop wasting time and start reading the book already.

the owners themselves, not affiliated with this document.

Chapter 1:

Introduction to Stocks

Let's be honest for a moment. Have you ever dreamt of owning a business so that you can increase your financial freedom and accumulate more wealth? But somehow haven't been able to do it and are instead stuck at a job with not so bright prospect. Because growing up, most of us were told that you can earn an income by working at a job. The problem with this approach is that there is a limit to the amount of money you can earn from your job. This depends firstly on the type of job you are working and the number of hour you are working. Of course, there is not much you can do about the number of hours. You don't want to work overnight otherwise you will get exhausted. You will spend all your time working and won't have the leisure time to enjoy using the money you earned. Then what's the point of working so much when you can't rejoice even a little with that money. True, isn't it?

But there is no need to worry. What if I tell you that you can own a business and work at your job at the same time? Sounds unrealistic? But it's not. It's closer to reality than you might think. In this book, I am going to comprehensively show you a way to own a business and increase your personal wealth. I would go step by step, explaining each point as plainly as possible so that there is not a bit of doubt left in your mind. In case you still haven't suspected, I am talking about "Stocks". It is without a doubt the best way to improve the personal expenses and accumulation of wealth. Although there are other ways of making an investment by putting your money into bonds, mutual funds, real estate and few others. But in this book, we are only going to talk about the stocks.

Stocks market fluctuates so rapidly that it is no less than a roller coaster. But of course, in this roller coaster we only want the ups and not the downs. Though not guaranteed, it's possible to swim safely in this ocean of stocks, without drowning. Through years of experience, experts have been able to come with effective strategies for finding good stocks. By explaining each of these strategies, we will try to raise your knowledge about stocks so that you can safely invest in it. We will teach on how to pass those gatekeepers and multiple barriers that have been built to stop people like us from entering this world. Some of these barriers are good as they stop uneducated investor from wasting his money. But investing in stocks has been unnecessarily made complicated so that only few selected groups can benefit.

But over the last few years, there has been an exponential rise in the average person's interest in stocks. The rapid advances in technology have made it possible for anyone to buy stocks with a click of the mouse. Having an interest is one thing, but if you don't understand the stock market fully, chances are that you might lose more money than gain from it. As opposed to popular belief about stocks, it is not a magical way to make money in a short span of time. Many people consider stocks as a way to quickly get rich without taking much risk. This of course is not true and this is exactly the kind of mentality you should refrain from. A smart person who values his money would first understand the stock market and get to know where he is putting his money in.

Before we proceed any further, we should put it out on the table that we do not have any magical spell that would make you rich overnight. The strategies that we are going to talk about are the best one out there but even they do not guarantee success every time. This is fundamentally because stock market is run by humans and humans are unpredictable. It is nearly impossible to every time predict a company's progress accurately because so many factors are at play simultaneously. We can find the quantitative information such as profit but it is really difficult to get authentic qualitative information such as company's staff etc. It is even possible that two opposing strategies can work at the same time. Such is the uncertainty.

But it does not mean that you cannot get rich. If you can learn how to interpret data, which factors to look for and some other things, then you can earn a lot from stocks with risking much. Now that you can paint a rough picture of how stock market looks and works, we will move further. This book will help you built a strong foundation you can base your investment decisions on. In this book, you will find everything you need to know about stocks; starting from the basic definition, its types, how you can buy it and much more.

What are Stocks

Remember earlier in the book I talked about owning a business. Well! This is exactly what a stock allows you to do. By buying a stock, you get a share in the ownership of the company. Technically they represent a claim in the company's assets and earnings. Yes! It means you become the owner of the company. By becoming the owner, you get rights and responsibilities such as the right to be informed to any changes to the company's future growth prospect and its risk of failure.

The stake of your ownership in the company increases with the number of stocks that you purchase. The more stocks you acquire, the more owner you have. You get a share of the company's earnings along with the voting rights attached to the stock. But owning stocks does not mean that you get a say in day-to-day operations of the company. The only thing you can do is elect the board of directors. This is because in order to have more influence, you need to have high percentage of shares which are mostly acquired by billionaire entrepreneurs and these people then make the critical decisions. As an ordinary shareholder, you get a portion of the company's profit and have a claim on assets. It means the more shares you buy, the more dividends you get.

A good thing about stocks is the limited liability. It means that in a case a company goes bankrupt; you are not personally liable to pay its debts. The maximum you can lose is the value of your investment; unlike partnerships where creditor can even come after the personal assets.

Before technology advanced and computers came, a person would get a stock certificate when he buys a stock. But nowadays, this record is kept electronically and is known as the holding shares in street name. Computers have made buying and selling of stocks very convenient.

Now before we move any further, let's answer a very fundamental question. Why Does Company issue stocks. Why does it have to share it profit with thousands of people when it has the option to keep all the profit to themselves. This is because when a company is doing well, it would want to expand and to do that, it would need money. There are two ways by which company can get this money; either by burrowing it from someone or by issuing stocks. In order to borrow money, a company can either take a loan from bank or by issuing bonds. In both cases, it is considered debt because the company has to pay back. You are guaranteed payment back from the company when you buy bonds. Now the good thing about issuing stocks is that the company does not have to pay back the money and make interest payments from time to time. Then why do people buy stocks? It's with this hope that the value of their shares will increase in the future.

The first set of stocks that a company offers is called Initial Public Offering (IPO). The company set a certain price per stock. The success of the company along with other factors will determine whether an individual will buy the stock or not. If he sees that the price of the stock will increase in the future, then you will buy that stock. The thing about dividends is that the company is not obliged to pay out dividends to its shareholders. So in this case, the only way you can money on a stock is through its appreciation. All these negative aspects, stocks have a great potential to give you great return on your investment; the greater the risk, the higher the return.

Types of Stocks

There are basically two major types of stocks; Common Stocks and Preferred Stocks. Buying any stock would make you an owner of the company.

Common stock gives you the right to vote for the board of directors along with a portion of the profit known as dividend. Most of the companies issue more common stock than preferred stock. They are riskier than Preferred stocks. In case a company goes bankrupt, common stock shareholders receive money after creditors, bondholders and preferred shareholders are paid respectively. But over the long run, they yield higher return than any other investment; so most of the investors chose common stock over preferred stock. Price appreciation on the stocks in the long run gives you more return.

Now let's talk about preferred stock. People who do not want to take much risk buy prefer stocks. This is because the price of the preferred stock does not fluctuate as much as the price of common stock. Unlike owning common stocks where you might or not might get dividend, owning preferred stock will always get you a dividend based on the profit. Preferred stockholders get dividends before the common stockholders. Similarly in case company going bankrupt, preferred stockholders has a claim to ay asset ahead of common stockholders. But the negative side of the preferred stock is that the stockholder does not get any voting rights. If this doesn't bother you, then preferred stock is the perfect option for you.

Different classes of stocks

Earlier in this section, we discussed the two main types of stocks. But companies use another way of categorization stocks into classes with in each type. So with in each type, they will divide the stocks into classes such as Class A and Class B. But why do companies do this? One of the major reasons is to keep the voting rights with in a certain group. It means that different classes of shares are given different voting rights. For example, a company makes two classes of commons stock; Class A and Class B. people who own class A shares are given twenty rights per share whereas the majority of the people who would own class B would be given one vote right per share.

Chapter 2:

How Stocks Work

How do Stocks are traded?

Say you want to buy stocks but do you know them place to buy them. For example, if you want to buy fruits and vegetables, you go to a fruit market. Isn't it? Similarly if you want to buy and sell stocks, you have to go to a stock market which is called Stock Exchange. This is the place where buyers and sellers meet and decide on a price that is acceptable to both. The purpose of this stock exchange is to facilitate and provide security to both buyer and seller. These trades could be physical where both the buyers and sellers are actually present at the trading floor or Virtual where trading is done electronically.

New York Stock Exchange is considered to be the most prestigious stock exchange in the world and the most preferred market choice for the biggest firms such as Coca-Cola, McDonalds, Wal-mart and many more. Nasdaq is another stock exchange which is more popular for virtual trading. Unlike NYSE, it does not have a central location or floor brokers. Trading is done through the high the highly developed IT and Telecommunications network of dealer. Many big technology companies such as Dell, Intel, Microsoft, and Oracle are all listed on Nasdaq stock exchange.

Now let's talk about how actually trading occurs in this stock markets. Most of the trading is done face-to-face on a trading floor in the NYSE. Initially orders are dispatched from the brokerage firm to the floor brokers who then go to a particular spot on the trading floor where the stocks are being traded. A person known as the "Specialist" is present at this spot and his job is to match buyers and sellers. Using the auction method, prices are decided. The price that is usually finalized is the highest price the buyer is willing to pay and minimum price seller is willing to sell. Once the trade has been made, the details are sent back to the brokerage firm who initiated the order. The Brokerage firm then notifies the investor who placed the order. Although much of this is done via physical contact, computers are also used in this trading process.

As mentioned earlier, much of traded on Nasdaq is virtual. They act as market makers for various stocks. They make frequent bids and ask prices within a prescribed percentage spread for shares.

Apart from these two Exchanges, they are also many other Stock exchanges not only in America but also in the whole world. For example, the London Stock Exchange and Hong Kong Stock Exchange are among the largest in the world.

Why do Stock Prices Change?

Stocks are highly volatile. They go up and down by a large percentage in a very short span of time. One of the way by which you earn through a stock is by price appreciation. It means how much value of a stock in terms of its price has increased over time. It has to increase by a decent margin in order to beat the inflation and cost of the taxes. The way the price of a stock goes up, the same way it can come down which is called price depreciation.

But what cause this increase and decrease in the stock value? Generally, the supply and demand is one of the forces that cause this change. Let's assume that more people want to buy the stock of a certain company than sell it. This means that the demand is higher than the supply and the price of the stock goes up. On the other hand, if more people want to sell (supply) stocks than buy it (demand), than the price goes down because there is more supply than demand. Pretty easy, right? But the difficult part is to find out why the supply of a certain stock increased. If you can know this, then it's easy for you to make future predictions that would prove right for you.

The value of a company is measured by multiplying the price of each stock with the number of shares the company has issued. Do not make the mistake of linking the value with just the stock price.

Earlier in the first chapter, we discussed how the earnings or profit of a company is positively linked with its value. It is common sense that a company has to make money or else it will go bankrupt. The more money a company makes, the better its reputation will be. To assist public, public companies are required to release their earnings report after every three months. These reports are then used by the analysts to make future predictions. But earnings are just one of the many ways to measure the value of a stock.

To be honest, nobody actually knows why the price of a stock increases or decreases. Investors and analysts have developed thousands of theories and indicators but even with them, it only gives an educated guess at the very best. Some even say that it is not possible to predict the future condition of a stock price.

Things to Inquire before actually buying Stocks

Now before we go on and tell you about the procedure to buy the stock, we want you keeps the following tips in mind that might save you losing your hard-earned cash. You should always ask yourself these questions before actually buying a stock.

As mentioned above, check out a company's earning using the quarterly and annual earnings reports. This would give you an idea on how well a company is doing. Find out what the company actually does. Many successful famous investors never invest in a company they don't know much about. So look into the company's operations and see how it works. This would give you a better idea about the company and reduce the risk.

Look into the company's past earning records and notice whether it has steady earnings growth or are they volatile. It's important to know who the companies' competitors are; every company has a few. See whether it's a big company or a small one. Is it an industry dominated by only company or divided among many companies? These question about company's competitors are important as they can give you can indication on how a company will perform in the future.

Check out a company's balance sheet and see whether the company is under debt or not. What do they do with the profit they earn? Do they invest it in research and future development? If a company is in debt, they it's certainly not a good idea to invest in it.

Research on the people who run the company. See whether they are qualified enough or not. A good way is to check who stable the management is. If the company has replaced lot of managers in a short period, then it certainly does not show a good future prospect. You can get all this information from a company's website or from publications by various industries.

These are the few things to keep in mind before buying a stock. It's also healthy to do a thorough research before investing you money into something.

Chapter 3:

Entering the Stock Market

Buying your first Stock

Buying stock is not difficult at all. There are two ways by which you can buy the stocks; using Brokerage firm and DRIPs & DIPs.

Using brokerage is the most common method to buy stocks. You can acquire their full service in which you will get expert advice and they you manage your account; but they also charge a lot for all of this. Secondly, you can get the Discount Brokerages offer, which is although cheaper, offers little personal assistance. You begin by opening a brokerage account with these firms. These firms usually send different reports on market conditions, either daily or weekly. You can do all this from your computer and save yourself from the effort to actually go to the trading floor. The time it takes to execute your order varies from broker to broker and market to market; but generally, it doesn't take much time and the price doesn't differ that much.

Another way which does not involve Brokerage firms is the Dividend Reinvestment Plans (DIRPs) and Direct Investment Plans (DIPs). In these plans, shareholders are allowed to purchase stocks directly from company for a minimal price.

Apart from buying and selling, you can also do short selling and buying. What you actually do is that you borrow some stocks and sell them, wishing that the stock will depreciate; allowing you to keep the difference between the selling price and eventual repurchase price in your pocket.

Different Stock Orders

When you buy your first stock, you broker would ask you about the stock order you would like to use. How would you tell him which one to use if you do not know it yourself? It is important to know about different orders. Fundamentally there are five types of orders you can use.

Market Order

If you place a market order when buying or selling a stock, then you will buy or sell a stock at the present market price which is almost the standard stock purchase order. But in this order, you don't control the amount of money you are paying; it all depends on the market. However, if you do not want to rely wholly on the market and want to set a limit on the amount, then you should use Limit Order.

Limit Order

This order allows you to set a range on the price at which you want to buy or sell a stock. It would stop you from purchasing or selling a stock at a price that is outside your range. But a problem with this order is that if the price too of the range, your order will never be executed and you wouldn't be able to buy or sell your stock. Brokers also charge more for this order since no execution means no commission.

Stop Order

Stop order is used when you want to save yourself from losing too much. For example, let's assume you purchased a stock at $30 but you know that the market is volatile so you set a stop-order at $25. It means that if the price of stock drops to $25 or below, your order becomes a market order and will be sold immediately at the best available price. But what if the price drops to $25 and then rises again, then you wouldn't have wanted to sell your stock. But there is nothing you can do since you placed a Stop Order. One way to overcome is to place a Stop-limit Order.

Stop-limit Order

A stop-limit order initiates a limit order instead of market order when the price of the stock drops to the targeted price. It has to hit the targeted price again in order to execute the order. For examples, let's say a stock opens at $20 way below your targeted price. A stop order would be executed by turning it into market order and stock would be sold immediately. But a Stop-limit order would not be executed since the price never touched $25 which was the targeted price. In this way it offers a greater protection.

Trailing Order

This is the last order which is a stop order based on a percentage change in the market price.

When you buy a stock and put an order, you also tell your broker how long the order stays open. If you don't do it, they become order by default remaining valid till the end of the day. You also have the option of good-till-cancelled orders which remain valid until you personally cancel them.

Suppose you put an order earlier and now you want to cancel it, you can do it as long as the order has not yet been executed. You can simply cancel it online or call you broker and ask him to do it. But if the order has been executed, there is nothing you can do it to stop it. So always think of all the consequences before placing an order.

Teaching you to read a stock

You need to know how to read stock in order to interpret the information make an informed decision. Otherwise it would just look of random numbers arranged together in a sheet of paper. You can get the stock quotes easily via the internet from the big financial sites such as MSN MoneyCentral, Yahoo! Finance to name a few. You just have to enter the Ticker symbol into the quote box on these website and the stock quote will appear. These websites update every day to equip you with the latest development.

You can even get charts, research articles on this subject.

If you look at a Stock quotes, you would notice that it is divided into columns. The first two columns are titled 52W high and 52W low. They actually show the highest and the lowest prices at which a stock has been traded in the last 52 weeks. Column 3 labeled as stocks display the name of the company along with the type of stock such as class. Column 4 shows the Ticker symbol which is actually a unique alphabetical which identifies the stock. Every company has a unique Ticker symbol. Normally, people search for companies using this ticker number.

Column 5 shows the annual dividend per share the company pays to its shareholders. If the space is blank, it indicates that the company does not pay out dividends. Column 6 which is the dividend Yield displays the percentage return on the dividend. This percentage is calculated by dividing the annual dividends per share by price per share.

Column 7 shows the price/earnings ratio. This ratio is very important for the investors and is calculated by dividing the present price of the stock by earnings per share by using EPS from the past four quarters. It is used to know the value of the stock. Companies that aren't profitable display a negative EPS and therefore makes it difficult to interpret. The average P/E ratio is the past has been around 15-25 but it varies greatly within companies and industries.

Column 8 is for the trading Volume which shows the total number of shares traded for that day. Simply multiply the number displayed on the paper by hundred or add "oo" to get the actual number. Column 9, Day High and Low, shows the highest and lowest prices at which the stock has been traded in that day.

Column 10 lists the "Close" price or the last trading price before the market closed on that day. If the closing price of the present day is higher or lower by more than 5% than the previous day's closing price, than whole listing for that stock is bold-faced.

Column 11 is labeled as Net Change which shows the dollar value change in the stock price from the previous day's closing price. If the net change is positive, it means that value of the dollar has increases and vice versa.

Chapter 4:

Different Investing Styles

Investing Styles and Strategies

It's obvious that there are many investing styles and strategies out there. Which one you choose depends on your motives, personality, and how eager you are to make money. Generally speaking, there are four different kinds of styles you can adopt and each one has unique name on the Stock Market; these are Bulls, Bears, Chickens, and Pigs. You will hear these terms a lot once you enter the stock market; so it's better to acquaint yourself with these terms.

The Bulls
Let's say you live in an economic era that is very prosperous; everyone is getting job, GDP is growing and stocks prices are increasing. Such a market is called Bull market. it's easier to choose stocks since most of the things are moving positively. People experiencing this market trend generally assume that the price of the stock will increase; such people are

called 'bull' and are said to have "bullish outlook". But such situation do not last a long time and prove fatal to some people if the market trend drops.

The Bears

Now thing of a market situation that is opposite of the Bulls market, a Bear market. It is an economically bad era where inflation is rapidly increasing, jobs are lesser, stocks prices are deprecating and GDP is not growing. Anyone who believes that the price of the stock is going to drop is called a "Bear". In this scenario, it is difficult to get profit from investing in stocks since everything is going down, so how to invest? You can wait till you assume that the bear market is ending and bull market will emerge. This way you can buy the stocks as a low price and then wait till the price goes up. Another way to play in this scenario is to do short selling which, as discussed earlier, is borrowing stocks and then selling at a higher price. In this way, you get the difference between the selling price and the new repurchasing price, after the price of the stock has been dropped. I may sound easier than it actually is.

The Chickens

The type third people are Chickens. As the name suggests, they are the people who do not take much risk and want to play safe since they are afraid to lose anything. This style does not get you rich which is what you want. In an effort to play safe and risk-free, they fail to earn lot of profit. Although it is advisable not take unnecessary risk, it is important to enter the market take informed risk if you want to get a return.

The Pigs

Out of all the four types, the Pigs are the one who take high-risk. They are those people with getting-rich-quickly mentality. They invest on stocks blindly without getting all the information about that company in order to get that one big magical score. In the end, they are the person who lose the most and that's why the professional traders loves these people.

These are the four major types of investment styles and strategies. The most important thing is to equip yourself with all the information before entering into the market. This way you will have a better idea about the type of strategy you want to adopt. Whatever you motive is, just try not to be the pig because they are the ones who always lose in the end. Both Bulls and

Bears can make money with the changing trend in the market; even the chickens. In will end this section with a famous stock saying:

"Bulls make money, Bears make money, but pigs just get slaughtered".

Diversification of Portfolio

When investing, it is always advised to diversify your portfolio; but why? Mainly for three reasons: firstly, it can help in managing risk, secondly it allows you to maintain a risk level you can bear and survive with, and thirdly, to maintain risk balance over time by rebalancing and reallocating your portfolio. An ideal portfolio will be tax efficient, well diversified, will be balanced between risk and reward and would protect principles.

The purpose of the stocks is not to increase the yield on your return; stocks and other investments can do that. Instead, it improves returns for a particular level of risk that you set based on your time span, your patience, targets etc.

Since we have talked enough about why you need to diversify your portfolio, let's talk about how you can do it. You can diversify your portfolio by choosing assets from different investment platforms such as bonds, stocks, cash real estate etc. Next you can diversify it within each investment category and since this book is all about stocks, we will only discuss stocks.

Diversifying in stocks means that your one stock should not make up more than 5% of your overall stocks portfolio. This is because investing too much in a single stock is highly risky. You can diversify it on the basis of the size of the companies known as market capitalization, on the basis of different industries and on the basis of geography or location etc. By doing this, you would save yourself from losing too much if a particular industry collapses since you can make it up from stocks in other industries.

Once you have diversified your portfolio by choosing stocks from variety of industries, the next step is to monitor it on regular basis and rebalance when necessary to maintain the risk level you can afford. This is to make sure that your portfolio is on the same risk level that you begin with and is following the same strategy. This is a long term process and you would be required to keep maintaining it from time to time.

In diversifying a portfolio, you can either adopt an aggressive or conservative strategy. In aggressive strategy, the investor aims for greater return but he also should have tolerance for high risk. On the other hand, in conservative strategy an investor makes low risk his number one priority. They generally do not get high return on their investment. Many billionaires would tell you adopt a defensive strategy.

You can divide your money into two categories. The first one would be low-risk that may not give you much reward but would assure a steady income. The second category would be a high risk in which you would try to gain the maximum return by playing aggressively.

Your portfolio should be devised in such a way that it should be able to beat the hefty taxes. Otherwise a large portion of your return would be deducted in the form of taxes and you would end up keeping a lot less than you should have.

Generally, there are three kinds of taxes that you should have knowledge about. The first one is the income tax which deducts a large portion of your income. The second one is the Long-term capital gain. This is applicable to all your investments that you have owned for more than a year and is fixed at 20%. The third one is the short-term capital gains. This applies to all your investment that you have kept for less than a year and rate is the same as the ordinary income taxes.

Your investment strategy should allow you to defer high taxes. Since we mentioned above how short-term capital gains can cost you so much tax, it is better to keep a property for more than a year so that you that you only have to pay the 20% long-term capital gain tax. This way you can save a lot on your return.

So in order to achieve your long term goals, you need to maintain a balance between risk and reward.

Chapter 5:

Most Successful Stock Investment Strategies

Proved Stock-Picking Strategies

Now that you are very much familiar with stocks, their different types, how to buy it and how to read it, the next step is to teach you about the most effective strategies in stock-picking. There are literally thousands of strategies developed by investors over the decades just to make stock buying easier. But even then, there is so much uncertainty that you can never know anything for sure and everything at best is an "educated guess".

There are many factors that make it impossible to develop a full proof formula or system for stock-picking. The stock market is run and managed by human who bring with themselves emotions and unpredictability. Emotions such as confidence and fear make stock market highly volatile. Secondly, although we can get data on company's earnings and stuff, it is very difficult to get authentic and reliable information on company's qualitative data such as staff, reputation, and so on. Thirdly, you never know for sure which factors are critical to company's success and which aren't; it varies so much within industries and companies and even contradicts on many occasion.

But despite this, these strategies do help you or assist you in other words in taking decision. The kind of strategy you choose depends on a number of factors such as risk tolerance you are ready you incur, time frame, time and energy you want to devote to stocks and most importantly your personal outlook. Are of these factors are the driving force that are crucial to your success. In this section, we might read terms such as Fundamental Analysis, Technical Analysis and etc. but don't worry; they aren't as complicated as they sound like. By the time, you will reach the end of this section, you will have a crystal clear idea about these terms and you will be practically able to utilize these terms when buying and selling stocks.

Fundamental Analysis

Suppose you now know all about the stocks and are ready to buy your first stock. You go online and check out a few companies but you are unable to know which company is better to invest and would yield higher return in the future. In this situation, fundamental analysis is the first thing that you do.

The theory

What exactly is fundamental analysis? In simple terms, it is a way to know a company's worth. Only when you know that the company is worth, you will buy its stocks. You do this by finding out the intrinsic value of the company which is basically the actual worth of the company in comparison to the value at which it is being traded in the stock market. You would only buy the stocks when you believe that the intrinsic value is greater than the market value. This is known as "fundamental analysis". The reason behind calculating intrinsic value is that the company provides value to its owner. For example, if someone owns a small business, for him the worth of its business is the money he gets annually once he has deducted all the expenses; which is basically the profit.

It's very easy to talk about the intrinsic value but how do you actually find the intrinsic value? The most common way is to add together all of its profit to get an idea of a company's worth. Remember to subtract the time value of money to get the actual worth. Many investors do not directly use this theory. Instead, they blend a number of theories and then base their decisions on it.

Greater Fool Theory

Greater fool theory assumes that people are rational and would buy a stock for more than its intrinsic value. But then why does stock market changes so rapidly and is volatile when the intrinsic value of company is static? This is where the trading of the stocks comes in. if people can sell a stock for a price higher than purchasing price, what do they need the cash flow for. This is one of the reasons why the stock market is so volatile because speculate about a company. This speculation in term causes the price of the stock to either rise or fall, depending on the kind speculation. This is the basics of investing in the stock market where you can gain a profit from sale of a stock by speculating.

This is why it's important to notice the trend and tendencies in the market along with its intrinsic value. If you rely solely on the fundamental analysis, there is a greater chance that you will be manipulated by the brokers.

This kind of analysis using which an investor relies more on the market trends than on the intrinsic value is called "Technical Analysis".

Putting Theory into Practice

There are so many "Ifs" and "Buts" when it comes to putting this theory into practice since most it is based mainly on assumption. Predicting a future accurately is nearly impossible since there are so variables and force. You don't know what's going to happen to a company in the next 5-10 years. Will it grow or falls under debt? Will the company's profit increase or will it go bankrupt? All of these questions pop in your head when you think about the future. Only when you can beat all these variables can you accurately guess the future; which is again very hard.

Qualitative Analysis

Qualitative Analysis, as inferred from the name, analyzes the non-quantifiable aspects of a company, most importantly its staff. The staff of a company can tell you a lot about how a company is going to perform in the future. The people at the top of management who make critical decisions are responsible for a strong management which ultimately reveals positive results.

Know about who is running the company such as the CEO, CFO, and COO etc. Do a comprehensive research on these people, finding about their educational level and previous employment. This background information will tell you how qualified the person is and whether he is suitable for the job or not. Find out answers on why he left his previous job and was it relevant to the industry he is currently working in. For example a person who has previously worked in the food industry and is now managing an IT company would raise doubts.

How does your company work

If you want to be sure whether you will get a good return on your stock, then you should know how your company actually makes money or in technical terms, what is the "Business Model" of that company. If you know this, then you would be able to able to calculate the worth of your share or your investment. If you keep on investing in some company you don't know about, you will always lose money in the long run. This is the mistake many people make; they blindly invest in companies on mere speculations and in the end, it cost them a fortune. There is so much information you need to acquire in order to know how a company makes money; otherwise "how a company makes money" is a vague in itself.

Company's Competitors

Remember we talked earlier about demand and supply. The demand of some product goes up when more people are willing to buy; this increase the stock price as well. If you are clever enough, you will notice that some industries have higher growth potential than others. For example, an IT or Tech industry have greater potential of growing than many other industries because of high demand. So even if there is medium company in this industry, it would give you a greater return than let's say a big company in a low demand industry. This is one way of knowing in which company to invest. Another way to know is by looking at Market Share; it less risky to invest in a company that dominates the market, for example McDonalds, Coca Cola etc.

Company's Reputation

Company's reputation among its consumers is of great value; it displays extensive marketing and market development. Investing in company like this actually diversifies your risk and can compensate for a loss in another stock. You know how popular brands such as Coca Cola, KFC and PayPal are. Their reputation would not decrease overnight; it even harder to spread false speculation about these companies. So investing in such companies seems like a good option.

Be careful about the companies whose reputation revolves around one person. Stocks of such companies are highly volatile since even any bad news spreads among the public about that person, it would destroy the overall reputation of the company; and you know what happens to stock prices of such companies.

Conclusion

In many ways, Qualitative analysis is far more effective in knowing about company's performance than fundamental analysis. Fundamental analysis only shows you data and there are not many ways to interpret it. Qualitative analysis on the other hand can present information from various perspectives and since Stocks buying is more of an art than science; it proves to be more useful. You don't have to be a research analyst to carry out all these analysis and identify a good company. Sometimes all you have to use is your common sense and you will see things working your way.

Investing in the Value

We have talked a lot about knowing a company's worth to see the potential growth. A company with a higher value will definitely have a higher worth. The key here is to look for companies that are trading in the stock market below their actual worth. In this way, your stock would have a more value than the money you invested and in the long run would yield greater result. Two Columbia University professors, Benjamin Graham and David Dodd, introduced this concept in 1930 and this is still being used by the investors.

Value investor analyses the worth of a company if it's get sold tomorrow. Companies that are undervalued are the ones that attract value investors because they see a chance of profit when the market realizes this and improve the value according to its actual worth.

Value investors have laid out some fundamental rules based on the relationship between present business price and some business fundamentals that they follow. They check out the price-to-earnings ratios (P/E) below a certain absolute limit, the dividend that they would get above a specified absolute limit, compare the book value per share at a certain level relative to the share price and total sale of a certain point relative to the company's market value.

It is important to know the difference between a "cheap" stock and an undervalued" stock. Otherwise you would end up investing in the wrong company and might lose money. If the price of a share drops, it may be for whole other reasons. Mainly it may be because the company is not doing well on the market and people are losing trust in it; which decreases the demand and increases the supply ultimately reducing the price. So you have to be careful in identifying a company that is actually undervalued.

You should think big because owning the right stocks can make you richer. There are many examples of people who just started with one share and are now the owners of billion dollar companies. These people focused more on investing in the right company rather than just earning off by trading. Since these people know the actual worth of a company, they are not worried by the daily market fluctuations and market volatility since they know these have nothing to do with the company,

You can find these value stocks on any stock market and in any industry such as NYSE, Nasdaq etc. You will have greater chance of finding these stocks in industries that have recently seen a downfall for some reasons not related to the operations and management of the company. Most of these industries are that rely heavily on customer's satisfaction such as the auto-mobile industry.

Room for error
No matter how accurate your predictions are, you should always have room for error. For example if you

think that an intrinsic value of a share is $50 and no matter how good your calculations are, you should always have a margin of error and put the price let's say at $40 or $45. Then if you find a stock at $30 a good bargain since it is still lower than your supposed intrinsic value. This way you will get a high return in the long run.

Growth Investing

Another strategy that is very popular is the Growth investing. Using this strategy, the investor invests in companies who have a high potential of growth in terms of both sales and earnings in the future. Companies that are seeing great demand and their demand are likely to increase in the future are applicable in this strategy, since these are the ones who have the high potential growth. For instance, take the Technology companies. May be if not today, in the 90s these companies grew exponentially resulting in huge returns for the company. But this strategy does not work every time.

This strategy is very different from the Value investing strategy. In value investing, investors focus more on the current unlike the growth investing where the focus is on the future potential. In most cases, companies are trading at a price higher than their intrinsic value in the growth investing. This is all in the hope that their value will increase in the future. Most of these companies are emerging ones who have the potential to rise in the future.

Now come to the basic question; how would you identify which company is suitable in reality for growth investment. To help you with this, researchers have set some guidelines for you to identify such companies.

The first way is to look at past earnings growth and see whether they are just normal or really good. You can either take the last-five years or ten-year's earnings data. A company who has shown good growth in the last ten years is more likely to keep showing this growth in the future. Next step is to shift from the past into the future growth and find out if it will show more than 15 % growth or not. Ideally, a company with future growth of more than 15% is considered a potential growth.

Observe the company's management and see whether it is competitive and qualified enough to maintain a higher growth rate. This can be quantifies using the "return on equity" (ROE). Then look if the company is maintaining costs and revenues or not. This is mainly discovered by checking out the pre-tax profit margin. Compare a company's present profit margin to its past margin and notice the difference. If this average is greater than the last five years, then it means that it has a good potential for growth.

The last guideline is to predict whether the price will double in the next five years or not. It means that there has to be a growth rate at least 15% per annum on the stock price. Only then the stock price would be doubled in the next five years.

Growth increases when something is being fed regularly. In stocks, it means to look for companies that are reinvesting in themselves regularly to improve their products using the latest technology and equipment.

GARP Investing

This strategy makes use of both Value and growth investment strategies. It somehow utilizes both of them to reach a conclusion. GARP investor simply looks for companies that are undervalued and also have a reasonable future growth.

They like to search for companies with positive earning numbers for the past few years and in the future. But they don't go for very high growth rate such as 25-50% as they consider it too high a risk. Instead they settle for a growth rate of 10-20%. Each GARP investor has a stock-picking strategy according to his own personal style.

P/E ratio is another tool GARP investors use. Since these people lie somewhere between value investors and growth investors, so they look for a P/E ratio that is higher than value investors but lower than what growth investors prefer. They prefer companies with P/E ratio in 15-25 range. They also prefer a low price-to-book (P/B) ratio.

Because of their strategies, they also get a return that is different from both value and growth investors.

They are less likely to suffer from unexpected changes in the market trends. But growth investor is likely to earn much greater return than GARP investor in bull market. In the bear market, value investor is likely to earn more than GARP investor. But the advantage of being a GARP investor is that you get consistent and predictable return without risking much.

Income Investing

As the term suggests, Income investing provides smooth and steady income. One of the most common ways of getting a steady income from stocks is by receiving dividend. Companies who are well established in the industry and do not require any more growth are most likely to provide dividends since they don't need to reinvest in themselves. Some industries pay dividends more often than others such as Utility.

Focus more on dividend yield than highest dividends by dividing the annual dividend per share by share price. This is the right way of knowing the return a stock owner gets on the dividend. 5-6% is the minimum yield most investors would like receive on their stock. You should know that dividends do not lower risk although it can be done by picking strong companies. It's also important to know that in most parts of the world, dividends are treated same as income and so are subjected to that same tax rate which actually lowers you final return.

CAN SLIM

C=Current Earnings

This strategy is dependent on a number of variables that are crucial to this overall strategy. The first word 'C' stands for Current Earnings which recommends you to buy stocks whose earning per share (EPS) in the most recent quarter have grown on a yearly basis; with a growth rate of at least 18-20%. Then it is advantageous to buy the stock of that company. It is also important to look on the other companies in the same industry and measure their progress. If the progress is good, then it assures you that the industry is doing well and investing in the company will bring you great return.

A=Annual Earnings

Using this strategy, you monitor the annual of growth of a company for the last five years and see which way it is heading. An annual earnings growth of 25-30% is expected of a suitable company to invest in.

N=New

The third demands you look for a recent change that the company has undergone which many experts think is necessary for company's success. It could be anything from a new management team, an increase in the stock price, new product or new market. it advises you not to avoid companies who have just increased their stock price fearing that it will come down very soon. But most of the time, this isn't the case. In fact, many who have increased their price very often keep a higher price; and even increase it.

S=Supply and Demand

The fourth letter stands for Supply and Demand which we all know how works. It tells when comparing one small firm and one large firm, it is relatively easier for a smaller firm to show outstanding gains; if all other factors are kept constant. It is because a large company needs to create a higher demand in comparison to small companies in order to display the same gains. If a large number of shares of a company are owned by institutional investors, then any major transactions made by these investors can greatly impact the share price. In contrast, individual investors pose less impact and are less likely to direct the company onto an undesirable path.

L=Leader or Laggard

This part tells you the importance to differentiate between the companies who will only give average return at best from those who have a great potential for higher return in the future. In this, you use the relative price strength by the stock price of specific company with other companies in the market. it should have at least a value of 70% which shows that it is above 70 companies from a total of 100 companies. Do not go for companies that are cheap; understand that they are cheap may be because they don't have high market demand.

I=Institutional Sponsorship

It shows the value of in companies that are partially sponsored by some large institutes. Ideally, a stock is a buy if at least 30% of its shares are owned by institutions. But make sure it is not overly owned by institutions, because in that case it wouldn't be profitable to buy that company's share.

The last criteria tells you to observe the market direction and see which type of market you are currently in; bull or bear. Make sure that you judge the market condition carefully by observing daily volumes and trend in the market

CAN SLIM is a very effective strategy as combines all the other strategies such as value, fundamental, growth etc.

Technical Analysis

What is Technical analysis? It has been defined by John Murphy in his book "Charting Made Easy" as

"Chart analysis (also called technical analysis) is the study of market action, using price charts, to forecast future price direction. The cornerstone of the technical philosophy is the belief that all factors that influence market price - fundamental information, political events, natural disasters, and psychological

factors - are quickly discounted in market activity. In other words, the impact of these external factors will quickly show up in some form of price movement, either up or down."

It uses past data and various indicators to predict a stock's price, relying more on the quantitative/statistical data. It follows three main principles: firstly, that the price always moves in trends, secondly, prices show reliable information and lastly, history always repeat itself.

This is a short term strategy that requires the technical analyst to take quick decisions. They make money by making use of the past data, charts and other indicators without knowing anything about the company which the fundamental analysts do. Technical analyst follows the market very closely and capitalizes on price fluctuations either by going up or down; unlike value investors who have to wait very longer to see the results of their decisions. If its prediction goes wrong, he immediately puts a stop – loss order. It means that technical analysts have to very quick at getting out of the unfavorable situations without wasting much time.

Technical analysts make use of some important concepts which are Support and Resistance. Support is when the technical analysts would expect the price of the stock to rise after a decline. On the other hand, Resistance is when they would expect the price of the stock to fall after an increase. They usually take a long position when it is the support level and a short position when it's the resistance level.

Although, the analysts make use of statistical data but the interpretation of that data is open to subjectivity as there is not any absolute indicator. Unlike most other strategies we discussed, it has its own rules and concepts it relies on.

Conclusion

In this book, we talked about and familiarized you with all the major strategies that investors utilize when investing in stocks. We tried to explain each strategy as comprehensively as possible so that you as a beginner to stocks can easily understand it.

Although all strategies are backed by years of research and experience, none guarantees high return yield on your investment; such is the nature of stock market. But this is also the thing that makes it more interesting and subjective to individual interpretation.

Take your first step and start investing in the stocks. Begin by investing a small amount to familiarize yourself with the practical market and the strategies. Because no matter how much you read about it, it is only when you are actually in the market that you can understand and interpret the different market trends and situations. Analyze your situation first to see where you stand and what kind of investment approach is best for you. And do not be discouraged if you lose some money because this is how it works in this market. Take some risk but not recklessly. But also avoid taking too much risk because that could be proved fatal; play like a wise man. In the end, we wish you all the best and hope that have learned about stocks from this book and would apply it into earning higher returns.

www.ingramcontent.com/pod-product-compliance
Lightning Source LLC
Chambersburg PA
CBHW070357190526
45169CB00003B/1034